Why Does God Allow Suffering?

ROBERT GRIFFITH

Copyright © 2024
Grace and Truth Publishing

All rights reserved. No part of
this book may be reproduced, stored in a
retrieval system, or transmitted in any
form, without the written permission of
Grace and Truth Publishing.

**All Bible quotes are from the
New International Version (NIV)**

NEW INTERNATIONAL VERSION, Copyright
1973, 1978 and 1984 by international Bible Society.
Used by permission of Zondervan Publishing
House. All rights reserved.

GRACE AND TRUTH PUBLISHING
www.graceandtruthpublishing.com.au

ISBN: 978-0-6486439-4-4

Introduction

At the root of this question we find the problem of evil which exists in a world which is supposed to be under God's control. This is how it usually goes: If God is all-powerful and good, then evil shouldn't exist. Nor should there be any suffering or pain.

If God was truly loving and all-powerful, He would surely do what was necessary to end all suffering, evil and agony in the world. But, if there is sorrow, suffering and evil in our world, then it must follow that God is either not all-powerful or not good.

Perhaps God is loving and detests all the suffering in the world, but His limited power stops Him from taking any action.

Alternatively, God might be strong enough to take action, but He doesn't really love us enough to end all suffering. Or maybe the world might exist as it is because God doesn't really exist at all.

But there is more to this than merely an intellectual dispute among philosophers. This is very personal. This impacts us all directly. We all have stories of how evil, pain and suffering have made their way into our life's journey.

It's possible that you have lost your partner, your career, your home, your health, a parent or a child. It's even possible that you've experienced terrible, unimaginable, unjustifiable evil in your life.

You may have experienced times when you were on your knees in tears, begging God, *"Where are you? Why did you let this happen to me?"*

My intention in this booklet is not to downplay or to devalue the anguish you may have endured in life. The Christian faith's ability to speak to the entirety of the human experience is among its most potent and exquisite features. You will come across many characters in the Bible who grieved and expressed their sorrow to God after experiencing tremendous suffering and loss.

Even more amazing is the fact that occasionally they even say how disappointed they are with God. The fact that God gave us all those Bible passages indicates that He is prepared for us to express all of our feelings to Him, especially when we suffer.

My desire in this booklet is to offer some positive news and remind you of the many different ways our compassionate God takes what was meant for evil and uses it for our good and His glory.

God is more than able to take your worst day and use it to teach, bless and transform you into the image of Jesus, which is His ultimate will for you.

The Origin Suffering

However, before we examine all the ways God can minister to us in and through our suffering, we need to make sure we are at the right starting point.

Many people get confused, even overwhelmed in their attempt to make sense of evil and suffering because they incorrectly assume that God 'sends' suffering to us as part of His purpose and will.

They believe that God 'allowing' something is the same as God 'initiating' something. They deduce that if God is all-powerful and all-knowing, He can intervene in His creation and stop such things from happening. So, when God doesn't stop something, it's the same as if He brought that upon us Himself. This flawed analysis has inflicted pain on so many.

When my children were growing up, there were a number of things they did which were not helpful and damaging to them and others – things which I may have been able to stop, had I intervened and forced their hand.

The fact that I didn't do that, does not mean I am responsible for or condoned their poor choices. The same is true with our heavenly Father and us.

The Bible tells us that when God finished creating the world and all that is in it, He saw everything and declared it was *"very good."* (Genesis 1:31).

There was no evil in God's creation. Nothing was wrong with what God made – and that includes us. Many Scriptures affirm that God is not the author of evil: *"God cannot be tempted by evil, and He Himself does not tempt anyone."* (James 1:13).

"God is light, and in Him there is no darkness at all." (1 John 1:5).

"God is not the author of confusion." (1 Cor 14:33) - and if that is true, He cannot in any way be the author of evil.

Occasionally someone will quote Isaiah 45:7 (KJV) and claim it proves that God made evil as a part of His creation: *"I form the light, and create darkness: I make peace, and create evil: I the Lord do all these things."*

But the New American Standard Bible translates Isaiah 45:6-7 more accurately:

"There is no one besides Me. I am the Lord, and there is no other, the One forming light and creating darkness, causing well-being and creating calamity; I am the Lord who does all these."

That is, God may introduce calamity as a judgment for the wicked, but He is never the author of evil.

Evil originates not from God but from His fallen creatures. By our own evil intention, then, mankind corrupted the pure nature we had received from our Creator, through our sin and disobedience.

We need to understand that sin is not a created thing. Sin is neither substance, being, spirit, nor matter. So it is technically not proper to think of sin as something that was created.

Sin is simply a lack of moral perfection in a fallen creature. Fallen humanity bears the responsibility for their sin and all evil on earth emanates from the sins of fallen creatures, and that includes Satan.

God is certainly sovereign over all evil. There's a sense in which it is proper even to say that evil is part of His eternal decree. He did not create evil, but He planned for it. It didn't take Him by surprise.

He declared the end from the very beginning, and He is still working all things for His good pleasure (Isaiah 46:9-10).

But God's role with regard to evil is never, ever as its author. He simply permits evil agents to work, then overrules evil for His own wise and holy ends. Ultimately He is able to make all things - including all the fruits of all the evil of all time - work together for a greater good (Romans 8:28).

So let's investigate this concept now – how God works in and through suffering and the evil which may come upon us in this broken world.

The best way I can do that is to examine three men that we find in the Bible: Joseph, Job and Jesus.

JOSEPH (Genesis 50:15–21)

In Genesis 50 we learn of an incident that occurred right before Joseph's death. I suggest that you take a moment to read those verses to re-familiarise yourself with this story before proceeding.

There isn't enough time to cover every element of Joseph's tale. For the sake of this discussion, I'll just briefly go over all of the hardships that Joseph went through in his life:

He was abandoned by his brothers when he was a small child; they sold him into slavery at the age of seventeen; he was wrongly convicted of sexual misconduct and served years in jail for it; and the only person who could have freed Joseph from prison had forgotten about him.

Are you able to connect anywhere in his story? Has a loved one passed away? Have you experienced abuse and mistreatment at the hands of someone close to you? Have you ever been falsely accused of something but endured the consequences as though you had committed the crime?

Have you ever thought your difficult circumstance was about to end only to have someone disappoint you and open a whole new chapter of torment?

A famine struck the entire region twenty years after Joseph's siblings had sold him into slavery. When his father learned that there was ample food in Egypt he sends Joseph's brothers down to fetch some food for the family.

They have no idea that the younger brother they had sold into slavery is now a government official in Egypt – and the one who is in charge of managing all the food supplies during the famine!

In order for the brothers to survive this famine, Joseph eventually orders them to carry their father and the entire family to Egypt, where they finally meet their brother.

The brothers fear that Joseph may seek retribution for what they did to him after their father passes away.

Genesis 50:18–21 *"His brothers then came and threw themselves down before him. 'We are your slaves,' they said. But Joseph said to them, 'Don't be afraid. Am I in the place of God?*

You intended to harm me, but God intended it for good to accomplish what is now being done, the saving of many lives.

So then, don't be afraid. I will provide for you and your children.' And he reassured them and spoke kindly to them."

Joseph refrains from doing two things. He doesn't seek retribution, recognising that God is the One responsible for dealing with his brother's actions, even if he does hold a very powerful position in the Egyptian government. Secondly, Joseph does not downplay their actions.

He calls it like it is when he says, *"You intended to harm me."*

Joseph acknowledges that God used their evil for good, saying, *"You intended to harm me, but God intended it for good to accomplish what is now being done, the saving of many lives."*

Joseph believes that if it was not for him, Egypt would not have had a plan to survive the famine, and he could have then lost his entire family. So, Joseph is now saving a lot of lives thanks to God, including his own family.

Here, two purposes are at work: God's grace and compassion, as opposed to and his brothers' evil intent. Now let's talk about Job.

JOB (JOB 1-2)

Among the oldest books in the Bible is the book of Job. Two of the first chapters present us with an unusual viewpoint and I encourage you to read those two chapters before continuing.

Job has a great love for God. He is the epitome of spirituality and godliness. From there, the text takes us into God's throne room. Around God's throne are spiritual creatures in a group.

One steps forth; we call him Satan or the devil. His name actually means *"the Satan"* in Hebrew.

Although we are not able to fully understand him or his actions, it appears from this account that he has been searching the planet for individuals who genuinely love God.

God then poses the following question to him: *"Have you considered that there is none like my servant Job on the earth, a spotless and upright man who respects God and turns away from evil?"*

According to Job 1:8, God thinks highly of Job. He portrays Job as a man who genuinely loves God.

"Well, does Job love you for no reason?" the Devil responds. *"Is it not the case that he loves you since you have blessed and protected him? He only loves you because of the excellent things you have done for him. If you take away those positive things, he will curse you in front of others."*

God then gives the devil authority to take good away from Job, as He declares, *"You will see what is really inside Job."*

The worst day of Job's entire life then follows.

He is first told: *"All of your donkeys and oxen have been taken, and the slaves who were in charge of them were slain."*

Before they are done, he hears from someone else that all the sheep the servants were watching over were burned by fire. Someone then tells him that a raiding force also grabbed all of his camels and slaughtered all the servants over them.

Another second servant then entered the room as the first was still speaking, saying, *"Your sons and daughters were eating and drinking in their brother's house and a wind blew it down and killed all of them."*

Job lost all of his children and his entire means of subsistence in a single day!

When someone called you, have you ever heard them say something like, *"You better sit down, I have some awful news."*

Have you had a day where you were just inundated with negative news? Have you ever had the feeling that life might crush you? So it was for Job.

Job's reaction is quite impressive.

Job 1:20-22 *"Then Job got up, tore off his robe, shaved his head, and knelt down to worship. And he declared, 'I was born into my mother's womb naked, and I will return there too.'*

Blessed be the name of the Lord, who gave and who has taken away. Overall, Job did not commit a sin or accuse God of being at fault."

He worshipped God in his grief and prayed, saying,

"The Lord gave, and the Lord has taken away; blessed be the name of the Lord" while shedding tears and being crushed by overwhelming grief.

However, things get worse for Job. *"Job still loves me even though he has lost so much,"* God tells the Satan, who responds, *"But Job himself was not hurt."* God once more gives the Devil licence to come against Job himself this time.

From his head to his feet, Job is then covered with sores. Job got a broken piece of pottery and began scraping them off while he sat in the dirt.

Have you ever experienced a medical emergency that completely upended your life? Have you ever been at your breaking point just to have something terrible happen to you?

Have you ever heard the words *"You have cancer," "Your heart is failing,"* or *"You have an inoperable tumour."* Did you feel as though all the strength in your legs was gone?

We can understand how Job's wife is broken by all of this suffering. Her spouse is now ill, her children are dead, their money has gone! What a horrible situation to endure.

Job 2:9-10 *"His wife said to him, 'Are you still maintaining your integrity? Curse God and die!" He replied, "You are talking like a foolish woman. Shall we accept good from God, and not trouble?"*

Once more, his reaction is astounding. Yet things are difficult for Job. He finds no purpose in living. When his three friends arrive, they sit with him in quiet while they grieve, but soon they begin to look for an answer. His pals think that good deeds bring rewards, and bad deeds bring punishments.

They assume that Job is being punished by God after observing all that is happening to him. They keep trying to persuade him to confess, asking, *"Job, what horrible thing have you done? Examine your spirit. Be sincere with oneself. What did you do to warrant this penalty?"*

But Job repeatedly responds, *"I am innocent! I did not do anything wrong to deserve this!"* He is very correct. God himself says so.

However Job is human, and so he is angry with God for letting him go through this kind of suffering and angry at his friends for making such accusations. So Job demands some answers from God as to why He is doing this to him. God does respond, but he never provides an explanation. He keeps Job in the dark about his suffering.

Instead, in chapter 3 we see God demonstrating to Job just how narrow his viewpoint is. In addition to showing Job around the cosmos, God poses many questions to him.

"Where were you when I established the earth's foundation? Do you bring about the sun's rising? Is it possible to summon lightning? Can you make the mind understand? Are you aware how the animal kingdom functions? And many more questions.

God is demonstrating clearly to Job that his viewpoint is constrained and that He is in charge of the whole complicated cosmos. Job discovers who he can trust but he is not told why he is suffering in such a way.

It is comparable to a father making a choice and having his child contest it. Maybe the child thinks it's unfair. However, the youngster's viewpoint is very narrow, and even if the father tried to explain his reasoning, the child would not comprehend it.

Rather than offering an explanation, the father just wraps his arm around the child and invites them to accompany him. He then lead the child to his tool shed where he demonstrates the many tools he is proficient with.

The father asks, *"Do you know what that does?"* pointing to specific ones. *"Are you aware of what this one is used for?"*

After the child responds, *"No,"* the father then takes them to work and shows them around his worksite, and inquire, *"Do you know what I do with this? I am the one who this person reports to? Do you know how this is built?"*

Maybe when they come back home, the father shows the child their retirement account, budget, chequebook, and so on. The child really doesn't understand any of it.

It's not the intention to make the child feel foolish.

Getting them to feel humble is the goal - to assist them in realising how narrow minded they are, that their father is handling a whole universe of choices and cause-and-effect realities that the child is not even conscious of. That's how God handles Job.

Finally, Job acknowledges God's correctness and bows down before him. *You have my trust.* Once more, though, we see that there are two goals at work: God wants to show that Job loves God, and Satan wants to show that Job doesn't.

This reiterates our main point: God has the ability to make good come from your sorrow. Let's look at Jesus now.

JESUS

Both Job and Joseph were decent individuals who endured unjustified suffering. But of all those who suffered the most, Jesus was the most innocent. However, Jesus endured suffering as a component of God's scheme to turn bad intentions into good, just like He did with Joseph and Job.

We need to take a much closer look in order to fully comprehend Jesus' pain.

Saying that suffering is something we choose is one way to respond to the question *"why does God allow suffering?"* We decided on a world of pain. When God first created the earth, it was a good creation. He created a beautiful place where His people could live in His presence while also being under His control, care, love, and safety.

He had forewarned Adam and Eve, the very first humans, that following their own path would end in death, but they still decided to manage things their own way. They made a choice to live without God. They disregarded God's sovereign rule over their lives, despite His clear warnings that this would bring death into the earth, and have terrible repercussions for mankind. Suffering has been a significant part of our world ever since.

We might react to that right away by saying, *"That's not fair! It's unfair that we should suffer as a result of a decision we didn't even make."*

Jesus steps in at this point. God sent His one and only Son, Jesus, to share in our pain because He loved the world so much. The Son of God took on the form of a man and went through human agony. Jesus always made wise decisions.

Jesus has always put His faith in God. Jesus never resisted God's authority; He lived under it all the time, even during His suffering. While it's true that Adam and Eve disobeyed God first, they weren't the only ones. We carry out the same action. Not only are we suffering as a result of their decision, but we are suffering because of our choices too.

That being said, Jesus is not like this. He paid a price for the bad decisions He never made. Jesus entered this world to bear the weight of our poor choices in order to set us all free.

The cross is the emblem of suffering that lies at the core of the Christian faith. Jesus went through His most agonising moment when He accepted the death that every one of us deserves for disobeying God. Jesus always said *"yes"* to God, but in order to atone for all the times we had said *"no."*

He gave His life as a sacrifice. Jesus always made wise decisions that we can now profit from. He will grant each of us eternal life if we give Him our life. He pardons us, restoring our connection to God.

Both God's plan and evil's objectives are revealed in Jesus' suffering.

Acts 4:27–28 *"Indeed Herod and Pontius Pilate met together with the Gentiles and the people of Israel in this city to conspire against your holy servant Jesus, whom you anointed. They did what your power and will had decided beforehand should happen."*

Jesus was tortured and beaten; betrayed by one of His followers; denied by one of His closest friends; accused of things He did not say or do; and finally exposed to the public eye while dying, naked on a cross – and all that in the final 24 hours of his life!

The people who carried out this action meant it for evil, but God meant it for good, for it provided the means for our reconciliation with Him and served as payment for our pardon.

We therefore need to always remember that our God has the ability to bring good out of our pain. When one person has a knife, they can kill, and yet a doctor's knife can heal. The actual instrument is the same, yet it serves two distinctly different functions.

Both will hurt. However, for one, that suffering and pain leads to death, while for the other, suffering leads to life.

God has completely healed our earth in eternity. In His heavenly kingdom, which one day will be the only kingdom we know, there is no pain, no death, no suffering and no heartache. But in this broken, earthly kingdom there is suffering at every turn!

When humanity rules the world, it is a world of pain; when God rules the world, it is a world of life, not death. Suffering allows us to loosen our tight grasp on worldly possessions and place our faith in God. It is clear that life without God is a death sentence.

As believers and children of God, we live in both kingdoms for now. Jesus came and ushered in the kingdom of heaven and He calls us each day to embrace His kingdom more and more. In the midst of our pain and loss, God calls us to trust Him.

When we are suffering, it is simple to think that we are superior to God and that we might manage the world more effectively if we were in charge. That belief is what initially led to our current dilemma.

Adam and Eve held the exact same belief - that we were more intelligent than God and could govern the world better our way!

When we are suffering, we need to have a trusting heart. Jesus went to the garden just before He was crucified. Along with a few of His closest pals, He went there to pray. Jesus anticipated the hardship. He anticipated the discomfort. He anticipated the death. In His anguish, He cried out to God:

Matthew 26:39 *"My Father, if it is possible, may this cup be taken from me. Yet not as I will, but as you will."*

Effectively, He was saying, *"Father, please allow me to choose a different course. Could this please be done in a different manner? However, I believe in you. I give myself over to you – so, not my will, but yours be done."*

Jesus understood the 'why' behind His anguish. He was aware of the cause. He frequently declared, *"I'm giving my life to save others."* It was difficult even with the 'why' understood, though.

Seldom will we understand the 'why' behind our suffering. Job was unaware of it. Perhaps even he reasoned that he needed that hardship to realise that God was wiser than he was. That undoubtedly played a role.

Joseph was always proclaiming his faith in God, even though he was unaware of the "why at the time. In the end, he saw it plainly.

We may not always understand the 'why' but we can have faith in 'Who' - that is, in God - Who has the capacity to bring good out of our suffering for the benefit of others as well as for ourselves. It might take us twenty years to see it, or we might not see it in this lifetime.

It's common for us to look back on a tough event in the past and realise that it was actually the best thing for us; this is known as the *"hindsight is 20/20"* effect.

Faith is trusting the *Who* when you don't know the *why*. Faith is bringing that retrospect perspective into the present so that we can say, *"I know this is the best thing for me because God loves me and God is good and he wants what is best for me,"* while the difficult thing is still occurring.

Now take a moment to list all the areas of your life where you have suffered in the past or are now experiencing suffering, or just think about them. Here are some things you should keep in mind as you ponder that list.

God is not distant from you when you are suffering. It is not a sign that God is neglecting you if you are suffering. Suffering may actually be an indication that God is instigating some of the most profound changes in your life, which will lead to the most amazing love, joy, and peace you have ever known. God does not reject you if you are suffering.

Those four words Jesus uttered in the garden that night are maybe the four hardest words for us to say in our life: *"Your will be done."* They demand that we give up our plans. They necessitate that we relinquish all power. They demand that we value the will of someone else over our own.

As Jesus prayed, we too can pray for the alleviation of suffering. In the end, though, we must admit that God's will is superior to ours and that we should seek it above our own. We must give up thinking that we are superior to God.

I have prayed, *"Your will be done,"* many times in my life but none of them more painful than the night I stood by the hospital bed of my 14 month old granddaughter who was suffering so intensely from Mitochondrial disease. I knew that God could heal her there and then - of that I had no doubt.

I also knew something of the intensity of the pain which my son and his wife had endured the past six months as they wrestled with their faith, their concept of God and their baby girl fading away right before their eyes.

I sensed God moulding me - my faith, my trust, and my character. I knew that God had not brought this wicked sickness into Lyla Grace's life. God is not the author of sickness, suffering and death.

This world is broken because of sin and each and every one of us only breathes by the grace of God. Sickness and death is the natural outcome of a broken world which is full of rebellious, faithless people. The fact that any of us live for any length of time is only because the grace of God is at work.

So I knew that God had not 'willed' for this baby to leave us so soon. But I also know that long before she was born, God had planned to use this baby's suffering to bless many people and I would need another whole book to tell you how many lives were touched and healed through Lyla Grace. God is always good, even in the midst of the worst that this world and Satan can dish out. Ask Joseph; ask Job; ask baby Lyla; ask Jesus.

www.ingramcontent.com/pod-product-compliance
Lightning Source LLC
Chambersburg PA
CBHW071848290426
44109CB00017B/1965